Covid / Corvid

Alyson Hallett & Penelope Shuttle

1

black black the water's ways   and
not   under a spray of finicky sun
with only a tatty toast for breakfast
slather of marmite   and o the lovely black paste
so salty unlike   this unbriny splash
of pouncy HaichTwoO
there are lions alive   in the water's
pelt and roar and if only
there'd been an egg   boiled or poached   a scarab
of gold in a coat of white   racing
downhill   grandad should have bet
on this instead of dogs at the tracks   sure to get
to the sea   salty dogs   no trace
of comings and goings   one drop squats
in two or three places at once   lovely quantum mutation

AH

2

whereas on the train I'm in two or three places
at once   or five or six or seven   mutation
of city to hill to field to bridge
but when will I step onboard again
fly for miles as if on the shoulder of a waterfall?

I'll not be riding no Pandemic Express any time soon
(and as for your marmite sarnie I'd rather go dancing)

lockdown mind takes me touring
a lifetime of stored-up pilgrim places
where the dead come alive
beside the waterfall
at Beeny
to admire the absolute vertical of white water
drilling down the air to the sea

PS

3

drilling down the air to the sea   were you
is that what you were at   bishbashbosh
no drill bit big enough to zero out
the pesky covid why's it so like corvid
clever buggers those birds   brain the size of a pea
but they're more synaptically adjusted
than many a   toree toree toree   i'd a notion
the earth was a   witch when i walked in the woods
earlier   saw her stitching the virus
into a net and casting it out   like spray from
a waterfall's mouth   a hoick of germs
on the back of a toad   you know how it goes
one iceberg to us   a few hundred thousand
humans to the planet   for compost
I'll show you   the earth might have said
vindictive   vendetta   oh what I'd give to be in a gondola
skimming along as if   nothing was wrong

AH

4

if nothing was wrong
I'd be somewhere else
visiting friends
in Ireland or France
not here under sombre house arrest
with a crow stood on my heart
waiting for me to wake
Brexit Brexit she croaks
as if this is all a joke
then flies off like a witch
back to the woods where
the waterfall is made of tears
the waterfall is made of tears
the waterfall is made of tears

PS

5

The waterfall is made of tears and
not enough tissues or toilet roll to mop
it up. Red nose with the rough stuff,
blotchy eyes, bags underneath puffed
as a cushion puffed with kapok.
The tree that speaks with the dead.
The tree that pours its roots into the ground
as if they were waterfalls and not roots.
Look at glass. It falls so slowly it slips.
Cowslips. Cows' lips. Favourite flower
in a field. Saw more flowers than
people in April. Spoke to the cows
they never spoke back. Trace and track.
The fever. The silence. Indigo.

Note: In Mayan myths the kapok tree was sacred. They believed the souls of the dead would climb up into its branches which reached into heaven.

AH

6

they never spoke back the silence
did they   those flowers   and cows
silence ran over the fields a pencil over tracing paper
tree roots dug in   trying to help
but the dead kept riding their hospital racetrack
living people never spoke back the silence
nor did the tears and tissues
the people of April stayed home they stayed put
didn't dare visit little bosky bits of Berkshire
or go down to Costa for an hour
afraid even of friends   were they friend or foe
the roads lingered for want of a car
the playgrounds lingered for want of a child
the world lingered for want of a cure

PS

7

the world lingered in the beak of a bird
that was not a bird   as it ripped
and tore into flesh   ppe shields the eyes
the nose the hands but what shields
the heart   what screens the hell of seeing
an impossibility of breath   in creatures
        designed to breathe
what is a wet sheet hung out   to dry
if it's not   a waterfall lifted to the wind
not even a virus prevents the migration
of waterfalls   splash your face and
the waterfall waltzes off with a flake of skin
        sewers and worst of all locked in
children   phoning   the Samaritans

Note: ppe stands for Personal Protective Equipment

AH

8

even a samaritan
crosses the road sometimes
leaves a sleeping child
beside the waterfall
now he's the waterfall's problem
and yet our samaritan's phone
remains in her hand
another child panicking
just breathe she says
take a breath
as if breath
is an alchemy
as if the world itself
is not dying for a breather

PS

9

Breather, brethren, water and stones, asphalt
and tarmacadam, trees, trees, pharynx and
larynx, trachea and lung. During nor-
mal inhalation, the diaphragm and
external intercostal muscles con-
tract and the ribcage elevates. During
normal exhalation the muscles re-
lax. Inside the lungs oxygen is ex-
changed for carbon dioxide. And the world
watched as a white policeman anchored his
knee on a black man's neck

watched the knee, the
noose, the ships, the sea, the whips, murder, death.

Note: On May 25, 2020, George Floyd, a 46-year-old black man, was murdered in Minneapolis, Minnesota, United States, while being arrested. Derek Chauvin, a white police officer, knelt on Floyd's neck for over nine minutes after he was handcuffed and lying face down.

Darnella Frazier, a 17-year-old girl, was taking her nine-year old cousin out for snacks when she stopped and filmed the police officer kneeling on George Floyd's neck. Frazier testified at Chauvin's trial. Her cell phone video is one of the prosecution's central pieces of evidence.

On 25th June, 2021, Chauvin was sentenced to 22.5 years in prison.

AH

10

2020's whips are old and new
they're whipping the world out of shape

the whips strut round Parliament
the whip cracks over the chief medical officer's head

whips snake over the choking crowd
the whips handle themselves with aplomb

never take a knee   believe history is on their side
whip up fake-news

mock the gentle whip of the soul –
the deathly whip-hand stomps down neck after neck after

no hill without gravestones no valley without a shadow
what shall we do brethren?

they say to dream of a whip
signifies unhappiness   ill-omened friendships

PS

11

A cough a sweat a loss of taste -
the virus arrives. The ill-omened
friend takes up intimate residence
and sets a table with forks and knives.
To be its host its air bnb or luxury hotel
is a destiny we've tried to avoid. Before long
it has trashed lungs overstayed its welcome
thrown wild parties and wrecked the human
tenement. Eviction is complicated.
There have been failures. Funerals.
Fuckwit political incompetence.
Fastidious hand washing. Terrible
guest we dream of outwitting you.

AH

12

fuck handwashing
fuck the sanitizer fuck the mask
fuck the gloves o ex-cuse me the fucking
fucking disposable gloves
fuck lockdown blues
fuck the fucking four walls closing in for fucks sake
fuck the supermarket queue   fuck the medical officers
fuck the cabinet the parliament our dozy crime minister
fuck washing the groceries in soapy water
fuck my outdoor shoes   fuck my indoor shoes
fuck my indoor clothes   my fucking outdoor garments
fuck the tories and fuck the fuck out of their fucking family trees
for ten generations past and for ten generations to come
in short   and let me make this perfectly clear   fuck

PS

13

Indigenous spiders. Three perfectly clear suns and a black leather slipper. Tuck the sheets around the bed. Dim glow of electric. A body surfaces from chemical sleep. What to keep from the otherworld? What to drag into committees, albums, warming ovens? A good loaf of bread, cheese, Peter Gizzi's natural history of tears. Who knows what crows think, or buzzards or ants? Road-kill reduced to zero for a few shimmering weeks. Empty car parks breathed. Cctv caught dragonflies shagging while water-falls poured their hearts over rocks and followed moon-slicked roads to the sea.

AH

14

the sea contains a serpent
who guards a treasure

her tresses green as the Indian Ocean
her eyes claggy brine-pits

from here to the moon
goes this serpent's lovely neck

and sometimes for the fun of it
mademoiselle turns herself

into a colossal underwater cat
prowling the wrecks

or even pretends to be a manticore
because she's tired so tired

of the tiresome treasure she's tasked to guard
the broken treasure called Britannia

PS

*

broken treasure Britannia
          following moon-slick roads   to the sea
                    let's make this clear
we dream of outwitting you
                    ill-omened
murderer
                    dying to
          phone the Samaritans
                              linger   cure
trace and track the   fever
          a waterfall of tears skimming along
as if   nothing is wrong
                              drill down the air
unlovely   quantum   mutation

AH & PS

1

Did that just happen?
                    Did a mason bee lay eggs in the hollow
metal tube in a chair on a balcony
then stuff it with moss? Did a government of
the twenty first century sanction driving sixty miles
to a castle and back as a way for their favourite
advisor to test if his eyes were working? Did the sky
strip itself of clouds for three whole weeks? Did I
dance in the Odd Down park-and-ride in a red dress,
did I walk in the middle of the road on white white
lines and live to tell the tale? Who is this haunting
the topsy-turvy screen? Some days I craved an ice-cream.
Some days I zoomed around the world. Some
days I knelt on the kitchen floor and wept with
the people in the radio as they buried their dead.

AH

2

people are burying their dead
as the world zooms and the pubs open

the world wobbles and the shops open and the cafes
and the schools and the betting shops
but people are burying their dead

the lockdown sails back
with its skull and crossbones flying
but the pubs are open and the distances are shrinking

and people are burying their dead
and no one is wearing the raven crown
and no one is counting the dead and people are at the graveside
but the pubs are open and the summer beaches are spiking

and the car parks are no longer for dancing in
and all the people are burying their dead

PS

3

all the people
said   do not scrape the bark
from the last tree   and the last tree said *all*
the dragonflies from here to Cheddar Gorge
and Cheddar Gorge
said *all the goats and sheep are running*
over the edge   and all the edges
said   *we are coalescing and*   *is it an ordinary*
Monday   Monday said *gravity's gone*
said *all of Newton's*   *apples are falling back*
into the branches of trees   the branches said   *pips*
are parachuting into rain   and all the rain
said *there are complex codes inside the mother tree*
fireflies cosmos feldspar
let the dead live   the complex mother said

AH

4

let the dead live   Neville Chamberlain is climbing a tree
why is the Prime Minister (May 1937 – May 1940)
climbing a tree at Chequers?
little-known fact   his driver recalls
Mr Chamberlain was an arboreal enthusiast
a tree lover and planter   his letters to his sister
consist almost entirely of tree lore and tree updates
it was a simple matter for the PM to scoot nimbly up a tree
saw off a dead branch   maintain the oak's welfare
or for the pleasure of meditating in a tree
sometimes when eminent visitors arrived at Chequers
they would be unaware that the PM was watching them
from a green and pleasant eyrie
ah if only Hitler had been a forester or even a tree

Note: For an account of Neville Chamberlain's arboreal interests and his tree climbing I am indebted to *1939: The War Nobody Wanted,* Frederick Taylor, Picador, 2019.

PS

5

Last night, walking by high trees in the
meadow with the dog as spaceship clouds
turned raspberry pink, one black crow
ripped its throat then heaved up a semi-
digested worm and deposited it in a teenager's
beak, so loud it seemed impossible for
such a scruff of feathers and hollow bones
to blast that kind of sound, and I've always
thought women should be louder, not quieter,
not gender-bound to whisper or make polite
snarlings in the corner, as if, crow, you're
showing us what it could be like if we hadn't
been burned at the stake or whisked away
in jackets designed to make us straight strait strait.

AH

6

Strait means *narrow, strict, constricted.*
Hence straitjacket, especially in ladies' sizes.

The economy is in dire straits.
We are in dire straits.

If a person strives to enter in at the strait gate
that person is seeking salvation of the soul,

wants to get into heaven, *explain'd and inculcated.*
But who believes that? Exactly.

The Strait of Hormuz is the narrow sea passage
between the Persian Gulf and the open ocean.

It is one of the world's most important choke points.
If it gets closed to shipping, the crows will pick our bones.

But back to that straitjacket… Available online,
durable, in a wide range of colours. 20 quid.

Note: explain'd and inculcated: Striving to Enter in at the Strait Gate Explain'd and Inculcated: and the Connection of Salvation Therewith, Proved from the Holy Scriptures. In Two Sermons on Luke XIII.24, by Jonathan Mayhew, 1761.

PS

7

I don't know where you're doing your shopping these days but the cheapest straitjacket I can find is on ebay for one hundred & four pounds & 26 pence from savannah georgia &

something
makes me
want to snap
out of the

page & plough
with a wayward horse
or knead
with dusty knuckles
while all the synapses mis-

mis- mis- fire

&

AH

8

&&
&&&
&&&&
&&&&&
or the horse
may snap
on this fine & dandy day
given the legacy
of empire
&&&&&
&&&&
&&&
&&
&

PS

9

the form can't stand up anymore
every scaffolding pole falls away

where will starlings stand
what will keep the roof against the sky

we will remember buildings as babies
remember hot red rooms that pulsed and boomed

a beforeness that dissolves as
icebergs or ice-cubes or edges of land

dissolve and what is this hotness
this climate climbing up the scale

as mercury climbs and fever, fever
I don't know if there are enough hands

to plant enough trees to mitigate
what might be our final migration -

AH

10

Here you are, on your hot little planet.
The world's finest gardening gloves
are planting oaks and sycamores, pines and chestnut trees.
The gloves are made of deerskin, but let's not judge,
even deer (sometimes) die of old age. The gloves
and the saplings are in a race against time.
Having feasted on the fall nectars, Monarch butterflies head north
on their four-generation flight, California, Florida or Mexico-bound.
They will roost in cloudy mountains all winter, or in other areas
that are privately-owned. Earlier migrants are more robust,
have redder, larger, longer wings than those at the tail end of the migration.
They do not disdain Cuba. Migrating reindeer can travel 35 miles a day.
They disdain carparks. You are here. There's nowhere else to go,
no pause button, no starship Ark. Take care.

PS

11

No starship Ark. No plan b. No hopping
on a butterfly's back and heading south
across the sea. No other planet waiting.
No ladder long enough to reach a star.
No car capable of driving to Mars. No
plan c or d. No undoing what's been done
or tucking into vodka and pizza to aid
forgetting. No oxygen except from trees.
No Earth to stand on if the rocks melt
with the sun. Dear dead deer, can you say
something from the other side? No answer.
No telephone to speak with the dead. Ouija,
mystic, third eye, big toe, little toe,
mountain, scree, yes, nowhere else to go.

AH

12

there are about 70 billion of them somewhere
the dead of the world since the world began
with their 70 billion smiles or frowns
perhaps they can't bear to drift off into the void
perhaps they're long gone and that faint sighing you hear
in the middle of the night (no need for a Ouija board)
isn't the 70 billion singing to pass the time but just your ear for the spooky
    is there time or place for the 70 billion? (I'm not bothering
    with heaven or hell because *duh*...)
    we'll join the billions someday   there's no getting round it
    we'll be the holy ghosts of us
    the last vestige butterflying round the globe
    in our extinction dance   the biggest congregation
    this side of the mountains of the moon

PS

13

Hard to believe there are mountains under
the sea. Diving bell holidays have not been
a good idea. Too cramped. Too stuffy.

Harder to get to the base than swim around
the summit. Pressure pushing you up
when all you want is to go down, to climb

into the blackest depths and wander
among meadows of frilled sharks, fangtooth
fish, vampire squids and giant tube worms.

Better known as seamounts these mountains
are volcanic peaks. They are the fire beneath
the tears, the words beneath the grief, a composite

of crushed and pulsing stars. In the far off world
of the world the hard and soft intermingle and
the sound of mountains rushes through shingle.

AH

14

when the rains come
they hit the *picos* hard as shingle

where there were no waterfalls
now there are *cascatas* everywhere

furious and full of the Virgin Mary
risen from those undersea fire mountains

to teach the world how to pray…
we've been assured

by our leader befrilled as a shark
our fang-tooth Tory

that Xmas is virus-safe
so (says the BVM) *Xmas is fucked my dears*

and so are you...
Pray

Note: BVM stands for Blessed Virgin Mary

PS

*

Pray

the sound of mountains
mountains of the moon
scree yes nowhere
take care
our final migration
&
&
colours
straits
a tree
the complex mother says
all the people
are burying their dead

AH & PS

Notes & Acknowledgements

This book began when Alyson sent Penny her first sonnet on 22nd June 2020.

On 17th July Alyson sent Penny her final sonnet. Penny emailed back on the 18th July saying, 'we've crossed the finishing line'.

The poems were written at high speed, in the white heat of the covid pandemic in the UK. At this point there was no vaccine in sight; we didn't know how long it would last or if we'd have another lockdown. People with covid were being rushed into hospitals and many were put into induced comas and linked up to ventilators. There was a shortage of ppe and endless stories of cronyism and incompetence in the Tory government.

This sequence of sonnets almost kept us sane when there seemed to be nothing but insanity and danger around us.

Many thanks to Jenny Bull for suggesting a trip to a waterfall which sparked the beginning of these sonnets.

Many thanks to Kay Cotton who provided a quiet haven for a day of essential editing of these poems.

LAY OUT YOUR UNREST

www.ingramcontent.com/pod-product-compliance
Lightning Source LLC
Chambersburg PA
CBHW031506040426
42444CB00007B/1230
9781913642549

Contents

How do you track and trace a waterfall, she said?

ISBN: 978-1-913642-54-9

Cover design by Aaron Kent

Edited & Typeset by Aaron Kent

Broken Sleep Books (2021)

Broken Sleep Books Ltd
Rhydwen,
Talgarreg,
SA44 4HB
Wales

COVID / CORVID

Hallett & Shuttle